MATH ALIVE

NATURE
MATH

Penny Dowdy

LEOPARD
LEARNING

Copyright © Leopard Learning 2009
www.leopardlearning.com

Created by Q2AMedia (www.q2amedia.com)

All rights reserved. No part of this publication may be reproduced, or stored in a retrieval system, or transmitted in any form or by any means, electronic, mechanical, photocopying, recording, or otherwise, without written permission of Leopard Learning, nor be otherwise circulated in any form of binding or cover other than that in which it is published and without a similar condition being imposed on the subsequent purchaser.

Published in India by Popular Prakashan Pvt. Ltd.; 301, Mahalaxmi Chambers, 22, Bhulabhai Desai Road, Mumbai – 400026, India for Brainworks Learning Systems Pvt. Ltd.
All rights reserved.

10 9 8 7 6 5 4 3 2 1

ISBN: 978-81-7991-502-8

Printed in India by : Azure Press Services, A-28, Naraina Ind. Area Phase 1, New Delhi - 28

STAR © STAR India Pvt. Ltd. The Starkids Logo and the Starkids creative Learning Logo are properties of STAR India Pvt. Ltd.

The photographs in this book are used by permission and through the courtesy of:
t=top b=bottom c=centre l=left r=right m=middle
Images&Stories/ Alamy: 4-5, Brett Atkins/ Shutterstock: 6, James Watt/ Pacific Stock/ Photolibrary: 8-9, Stephen Frink Collection / Alamy: 8bl, Gelpi/ Shutterstock: 10, Louie Psihoyos/ Getty Images: 13, Mark Garlick/ Science Photo Library/ Photolibrary: 14-15, Todd Marshall: 16, William J. Mahnken/ Shutterstock: 18-19, Thorsten Rust/ Shutterstock: 19tr, Salihguler /Istockphoto: 20bl, Petr Nad/ Shutterstock: 20-21, Gianna Stadelmyer/Dreamstime: 22, Astrofoto/ Photolibrary: 25, Jurgen Ziewe/Shutterstock: 26-27, Mikhail Lavrenov/ Istockphoto: 28.
Illustrations: Q2AMedia Art Bank

Cover Photo: Front: Shutterstock. Back: UltraOrto, S.A./Shutterstock.
Half Title: Gelpi/ Shutterstock.
Creative Director: Simmi Sikka
Series Editor: Jessica Cohn
Art Director: Sudakshina Basu
Designers: Joita Das and Prashant Kumar
Illustrators: Indranil Ganguly, Rishi Bhardwaj, Kusum Kala and Pooja Shukla
Photo research: Sejal Sehgal
Senior Project Manager: Ravneet Kaur
Project Manager: Shekhar Kapur

Contents

Nature of Numbers	**4**
Nature's Numbers in Bees	6
Nothing to Sneeze at	8
Numbers in Nature	10
Circle of Life	12
Geometry and Nature	**14**
Crystal Clear	16
Snow Crystals	18
Symmetry in Nature	20
Weather or Not	**22**
Tools of Weaqther	24
Severe Weather	26
Weather Myths	28
Glossary	30
Answer Key	31
Index	32

Nature of Numbers

Way back in the early 1200s, a mathematician named **Fibonacci** studied how numbers occur in **patterns** in nature. The things that he realized then are still astounding people today.

Too Many Bunnies

In one instance, Fibonacci studied rabbits. Rabbits can start reproducing at one month old. If a pair of rabbits creates another pair of rabbits every month, how many pairs of rabbits would there be at the end of a year? This would not happen in real life. Fibonacci was interested in the numbers and their patterns, not the rabbits. Here is a table that shows what he found:

Month	Rabbits	Pairs	
1	AA	1	This is the first pair of rabbits. They are not a month old, so they can't mate yet.
2	AA	1	These rabbits are old enough to mate.
3	AA→BB	2	Pair A has babies, Pair B.
4	AA→BB →CC	3	Pair A has another set of babies, Pair C. Pair B is still too young to mate.
5	AA→BB→DD →CC →EE	5	Pair A has another set of babies, Pair E. Pair B has babies, too, Pair D. Pair C is still too young to mate.
6	AA→BB→DD ↓→FF →CC→GG →EE →HH	8	Pair A has another set of babies, Pair H. Pair B has another set of babies, Pair F. Pair C has babies, Pair G. Pair E is too young to mate.

At this point, you may think that there would be fifteen or twenty pairs at the end of the year. However, if you continue these patterns, there would be a whopping 144 pairs of rabbits!

Calculation Station

Look at the number of pairs in the table, and read the number of pairs from top to bottom:

1, 1, 2, 3, 5, 8, . . .

What is the pattern for these numbers? Hint: What happens if you add the first and second number? What about the second and third? (Answer is on page 31.)

▲ Rabbits do not always have litters in pairs. Yet the Fibonacci sequence does occur a lot in nature.

Nature's Numbers in Bees

As it turns out, that pattern of numbers (1, 1, 2, 3, 5, 8 . . .) repeats throughout nature. The pattern became known as the **Fibonacci sequence**.

The honeybee family tree is another example of the Fibonacci sequence. Each hive has one queen, who gets special treatment. The queen dines on royal jelly, a substance made only by very young bees. A female baby cannot become the queen unless she is fed lots of royal jelly from the start.

Female queen bees have to mate with a male bee to have female bees. Yet queen bees can have male bees without mating at all. So while every female bee has two parents, each male bee only has one. Let's look at the male bee's family tree, backward, and see what it has to do with Fibonacci.

▼ One male bee has one parent and two grandparents. There are three great-grandparents. There are five great-great-grandparents: 1, 1, 2, 3, 5. These numbers represent the Fibonacci sequence.

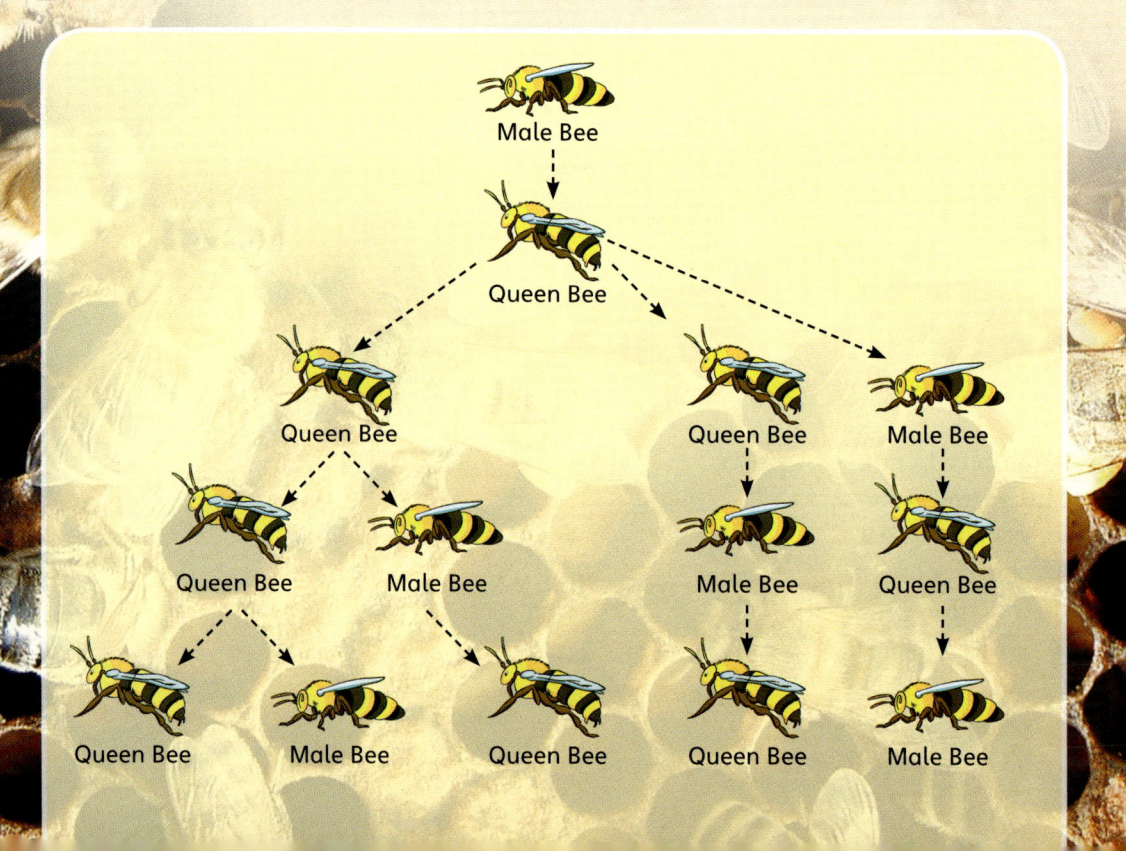

Hands-On Math: Boy Bees

Look again at the male bee's family tree, as it goes backward. Then try drawing a backward tree for his mother. Show the queen bee family tree back to her great-grandparents.

What You Will Need:
- Paper
- Pen or Pencil

What to Do:

1 Create the family tree for the queen bee.

2 Remember that male bees only have one parent, but queen bees have two.

3 The family tree should have five rows.

Explain Away
Are the numbers related to the Fibonacci sequence? Explain your thinking. (Answers are on page 31.)

Nothing to Sneeze at

Fibonacci's numbers appear in many places in nature once you start looking for them. Look at the white flowers on the page. They are the flowers of the sneezewort. The chart at the bottom of the page shows a flat line for each point where a new branch grows. Count the stems where each line touches. Look for the Fibonacci sequence: 1, 1, 2, 3, 5.

Patterns in Bloom

The Fibonacci sequence appears in other plants as well. Consider the sunflower and how its leaves appear along the stem from the top down to the ground. The first leaf is very near the flower bud. The second leaf grows below the first leaf but on a different side of the stem. This continues all the way down the stem.

If you look downward at the sunflower and turn it, you will count three leaves on the stem before you come back to the original position. On the second turn there are five leaves. Go around again, and there are eight leaves. The number of leaves you count on the turns —3, 5, 8— are part of the Fibonacci sequence. If you continue down the stem, more numbers of the sequence appear.

Sneezewort Pattern

Mathematicians believe that most plants grow with this pattern. It is smart way to grow! It helps each new leaf gets sun and water without being blocked by older leaves.

▼ The sneezewort shows the Fibonacci sequence.

Calculation Station

You get 3, 5, and 8 leaves in the first three turns of a sunflower stem. How many leaves would you expect to find the fourth, fifth, and sixth turn of a sunflower's stem? (Hint: If you need help, turn the page.) (Answer is on page 31.)

Numbers in Nature

Many mathematicians find the Fibonacci sequence fascinating because it occurs so often. In nature, numbers from the sequence appear apart from the sequence, too. When mathematicians call a number a Fibonacci number, they are referring to any number that appears in the Fibonacci sequence. Look at the numbers in the Fibonacci sequence to the right:

The number 610 is a Fibonacci number because it is part of the sequence. So is 6,765. Fibonacci numbers are found in many places. Cut open a banana crosswise. You will see three sections—a Fibonacci number. Cut open an apple and you will see five sections. Count the petals on many flowers and you will find Fibonacci numbers.

There are flowers that have 55 and 89 petals.

▼ Which petals and leaves show the 1, 2, 3, 5, 8, 13, 21, 34 pattern?

Number of Petals	Flower
3	lily, iris
5	buttercup, wild rose, larkspur, columbine
8	Delphinium
13	corn marigold
21	black-eyed Susan

Hands-On Math: Nature's Pattern

Take a look at these foods and find their Fibonacci numbers.

What You Will Need:
- Cucumber
- Green Pepper
- Lemon
- Tomato
- Pear
- Knife for adult to use

What to Do:

1 Have an adult cut open each of the foods crosswise.

2 Examine the inside sections of the foods.

3 List the ways that these foods show a Fibonacci number.

Explain Away
What other common plants can you find that have Fibonacci numbers? Explore your yard or a local park to find an answer. Do not pick the flowers in a park— just look at them. (Answers are on page 31.)

Circle of Life

Many things in nature are arranged in a **spiral**. Look closely at the seed head of the sunflower.

The seeds are in two spiral patterns. Look carefully. There is a clockwise spiral of seeds, going to the right. There is a counterclockwise spiral of seeds, going to the left. If you count the clockwise spirals, you will count 55 curving rows. If you count the counterclockwise spirals, you will count 89 curved rows. Not only are those Fibonacci numbers, but they are right next to each other in the sequence and in the flower!

Seed Pattern

Spirals Everywhere!

The two-direction spirals can be found on the outsides of pineapples, too. The spirals are found in the clusters of cauliflowers. They also appear in the arrangement of seeds on many other flowers. Scientists think that this design allows a plant to grow the greatest number of seeds or leaves possible.

▼ In the sunflower, seeds grow at the center and move outward.

Calculation Station

Find a pine cone and look on the underside. Find the two spirals. How many clockwise spirals are there? How many counterclockwise spirals are there? (Answer is on page 31.)

Geometry and Nature

Simple shapes, like the rings on a tree trunk, are everywhere in nature. Others are complicated. Take honeycombs, for example. Honeybees display some interesting shapes in their homes. They create **tessellations** out of **regular hexagons**.

Back to the Bees

What is a tessellation? What are regular hexagons? What do they have to do with honeybees?

A **regular polygon** is a shape with sides of the same length and angles of the same measure. A hexagon has six sides, so a regular hexagon has six sides that are all the same length. It also has six angles with the same measure.

Look at a honeycomb. See how the hexagons all fit against each other without any gaps or overlaps. This is a tessellation. It works like tiles on a floor, in some ways. The entire space of the honeycomb is covered with hexagons with no spaces between them.

Tessellations also appear elsewhere in nature. Even the patterns created by cracking ice or mud can be tessellations.

▼ No space is wasted in a honeycomb.

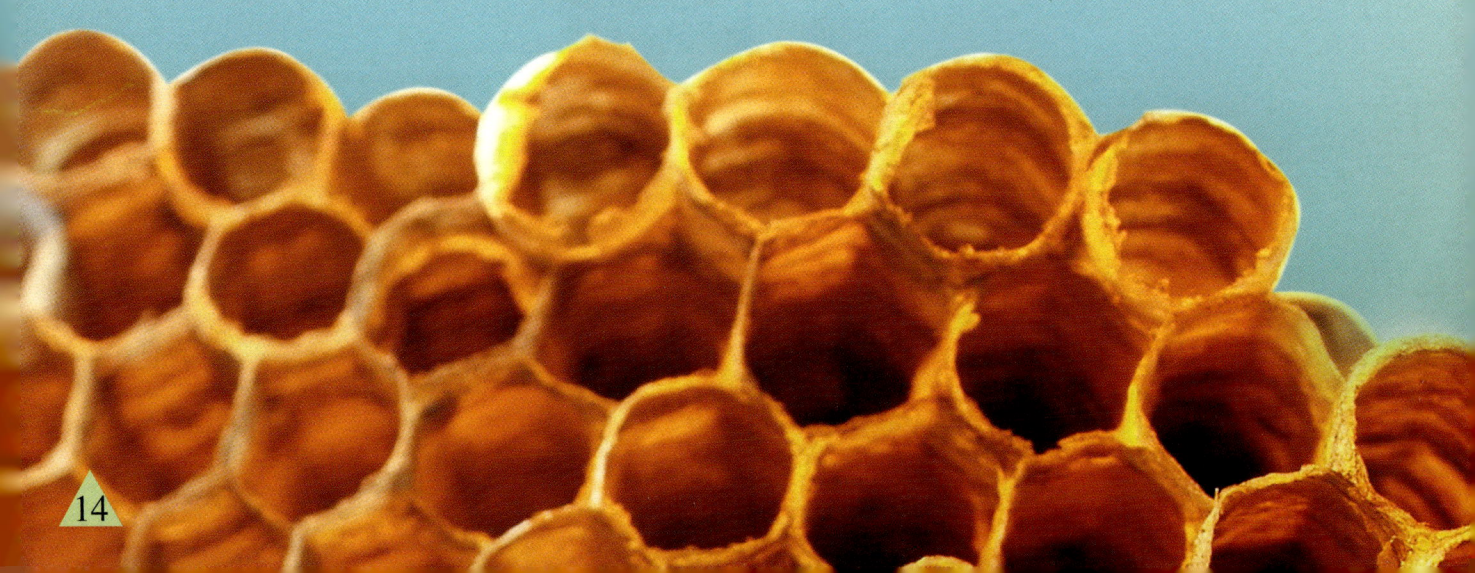

Hands-On Math: Tessellation

Irregular figures can make beautiful tessellations.

What You Will Need:
- Small square sheet of stiff paper or card stock
- Scissors • Tape
- Large sheet of drawing paper

What to Do:

1 Cut from the lower right corner to the upper right corner.

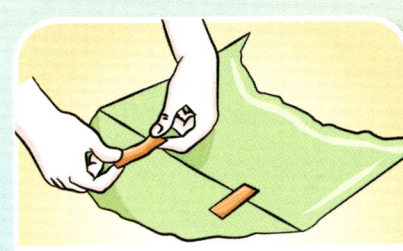

2 Slide the cut piece to the left. Tape flat sides together.

3 Cut from the original upper left corner to the upper right.

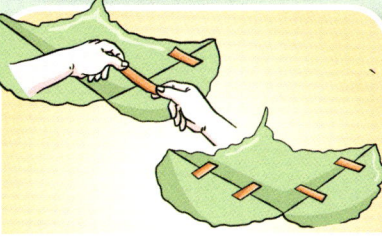

4 Slide that piece to the bottom. Tape from corner to corner.

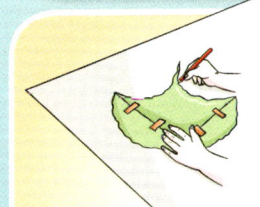

5 Trace the shape on the big paper. Then fit the shape to the tracing.

6 Repeat Step 5 until your page is filled. Color the drawing.

Explain Away
How did you make your shape fit the tessellation?

Crystal Clear

Tessellations appear to be flat. Other kinds of shapes take up space, and these shapes are called **three-dimensional**. They have length, width, and height. Some three-dimensional shapes are very simple, such as a shoebox. Others, such as **crystals**, are much more complicated.

Crystals form when certain compounds melt, cool slowly, and harden. To understand how that happens, it is important to learn about **molecules**. Molecules are the smallest units of a compound that have the same properties as the compound. In other words, these units would have the same properties even if each unit were on its own. Because the molecules of a compound are the same, the shapes of the compound's crystals end up the same. Let's see how that works with gold and emeralds.

Gold and Emeralds

Gold forms a crystal in the shape of a **cube**. A cube has six sides, or faces. Each of the flat sides is a square. Every gold crystal looks the same as every other gold crystal.

Emeralds are **hexagonal crystals**. They have eight sides, or faces. An emerald has two ends that are hexagons. The two ends of the emerald are connected by six rectangles. Every emerald crystal is made the same way.

Scientists have found only seven basic shapes of all crystals in nature. Every substance that can form a crystal makes one of these basic shapes. (The names are complicated, but the shapes are all simple.)

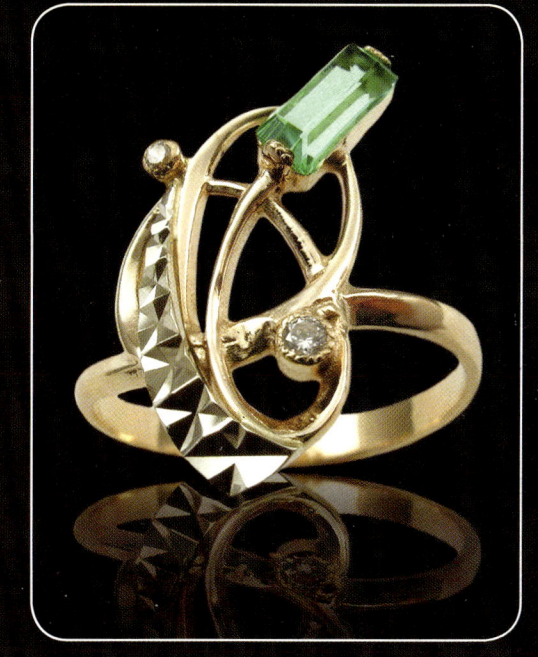

▲ The green gem is an emerald.

Type of Crystal	Number of Faces	Shapes of Faces
cubic	6	all squares
tetragonal	6	four rectangles and two squares
orthorhombic	6	all rectangles
rhombohedral	6	all rhombi (parallelograms with all four sides of equal length)
monoclinic	6	four rectangles and two parallelograms
triclinic	6	all parallelograms
hexagonal	8	two hexagons and six rectangles

▼ The amethyst is a hexagonal crystal.

Calculation Station

You know what a basketball or a fishing net is. Yet a net in math is different. A net in math is a three-dimensional shape laid flat. It looks like the shape has been unfolded.

Play around with that thought. Try drawing a net of a cubic, or six-sided, crystal. Then try drawing a net of a hexagonal crystal. (Hint: There should be one shape in the net for each side of the crystal.) (Answer is on page 31.)

Snow Crystals

When water freezes, ice crystals can form. Ice crystals are the same shape as emeralds—hexagons on the ends with rectangles connecting them. Snowflakes are made of ice crystals. So why aren't all snowflakes shaped the same?

Snowflakes all have a center with hexagon-shaped ends. Yet as a snowflake falls through the sky, it can start branching off each of its six corners. These branches can then make branches. That branching continues until the snowflake lands on the ground.

Branching Out—or Not

There are snowflakes that look like plates. There are snowflakes that look like trees. Some even end up looking like columns or needles, because branches never form. All snowflakes are different. Yet the basic shape at their center is still a hexagon, because all ice crystals are hexagon-shaped.

Snow from a snow-making machine doesn't feel like the real thing. Part of the reason is that drops of water spray from the machine. The drops freeze quickly. So crystals don't have a chance to form. This snow is made of frozen drops instead of frozen ice crystals. Frozen drops are shaped differently from snow that falls from the sky, even though both start out as water.

◀ Snowflakes branch in six directions.

Hands-On Math: Snowflakes in Two Dimensions

You can create two-dimensional models of three-dimensional snowflakes.

What You Will Need:
- Heavy book
- Paper coffee filter with flat bottom, or basket style
- Scissors

What to Do:

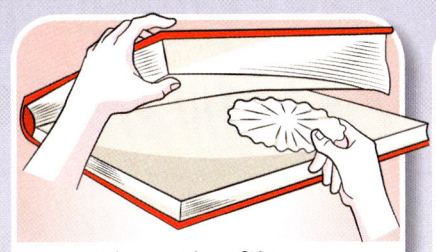

1 Place the filter inside a heavy book to flatten out overnight.

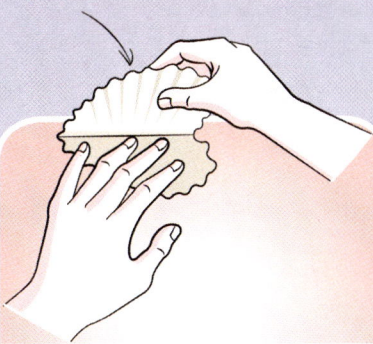

2 The next day, fold the filter in half.

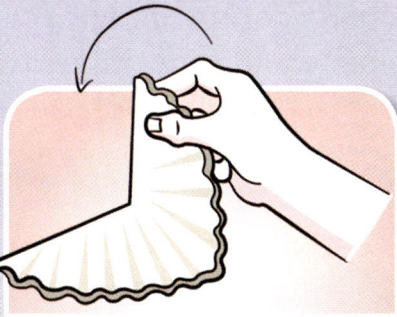

3 Fold the half-circle in thirds.

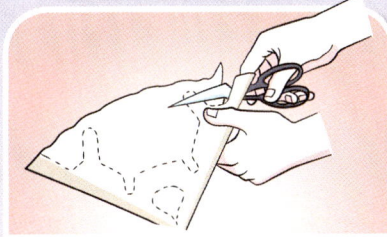

4 Make cuts on the sides. Make sure some of the folds remain.

5 Unfold and enjoy.

Explain Away
Why did you have to fold the paper in thirds instead of in half again? (Answer is on page 31.)

Symmetry in Nature

Nature shows examples of **symmetry**. That is when different sides look the same. Some objects or animals have **reflectional symmetry**. That means that if someone drew a line through that object or animal, one side of the line would reflect the other. Some objects or animals have **rotational symmetry**. What is that? If you look at the object and then turn it, the way you turn the knob on a sink, the image repeats.

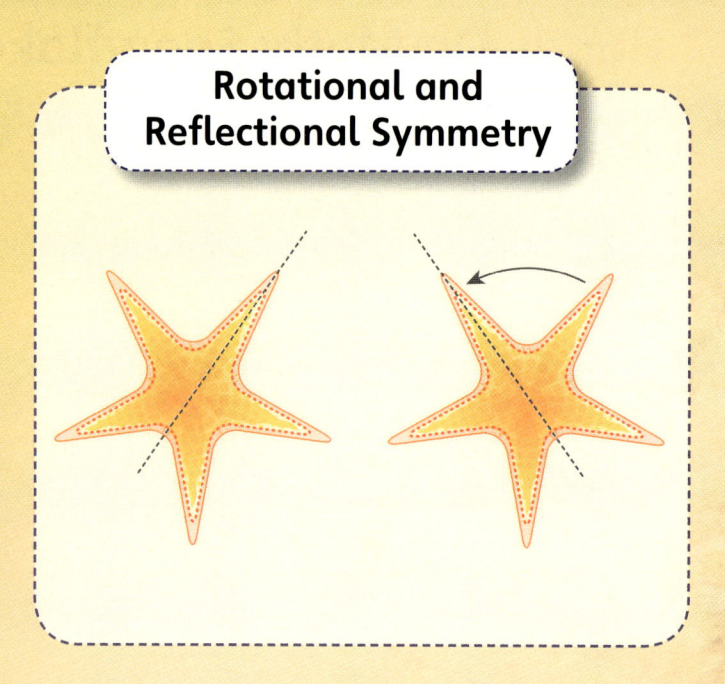

Rotational and Reflectional Symmetry

▲ Look for patterns in petals and leaves.

Folds and Turns

A butterfly has reflectional symmetry. Draw an imaginary line down the center of its body, and "fold" the butterfly on that line. The butterfly's wings line up on each other, as do its legs and eyes. Many animals have reflectional symmetry; even humans do. A fiddler crab, with one claw much larger than the other, is one example of an animal that does not have reflectional symmetry.

A starfish has rotational symmetry. Turn the starfish one-fifth of a turn to the right or left, and all parts of the animal line up again. In fact, the starfish has both reflectional and rotational symmetry. Draw an imaginary line to divide the starfish into two halves. Each half would be a reflection of the other.

Calculation Station

Go to your yard or a local park. What natural items can you find that have reflectional symmetry? Rotational symmetry? (Answers are on page 31.)

▼ In different seasons, you can find different specimens.

Weather or Not

People depend on weather forecasts. Will you need an umbrella today? Should you dress in layers to be prepared for cold weather or dress lightly for a warm day?

Making Predictions

Predicting the weather is not exact. Forecasters use **probability** to describe what they predict will happen. Scientists look at current weather patterns to make forecasts. They also study records from earlier years.

For example, let's say that winds have changed direction and clouds have moved in. Scientists study records from other times when that pattern showed up. Then they decide what is most likely to happen.

If there is a 20 percent chance of rain, that means forecasters looked at days that had weather very similar to this day. On 20 percent of those days, it rained.

◄ A weather prediction is an educated guess.

Hands-On Math: Data Tracker

Weather forecasters must keep detailed records to help them predict the weather. You can track the weather, too.

What You Will Need:
- Outdoor thermometer
- Pen or Pencil
- Paper

What to Do:

1 Measure the temperature outside at 7 a.m. and 7 p.m. for seven days.

2 Record the temperature in a table like the one on this page.

	TEMPERATURES	
DAY 1	7 AM.:	7 PM.:
DAY 2	7 AM.:	7 PM.:
DAY 3	7 AM.:	7 PM.:
DAY 4	7 AM.:	7 PM.:
DAY 5	7 AM.:	7 PM.:
DAY 6	7 AM.:	7 PM.:
DAY 7	7 AM.:	7 PM.:

Explain Away
What do you think the temperatures will be on Day 8? Explain your thinking. (Answer is on page 31.)

Tools of Weather

Weather forecasting has changed over time. Before computers, weather **satellites**, and **Doppler radar**, scientists used the following instruments. Most of these are still used today along with the more advanced tools:

- **Anemometers** measure wind speed.
- Thermometers measure temperature.
- A **rain gauge** collects rainwater and measures how much rain has fallen.
- A **hygrometer** measures humidity, or how much water is in the air.
- A **barometer** measures air pressure.

When the air pressure is low, the weather can be stormy. When the pressure is high, the weather tends to be pleasant. Together, the five measurement tools make a **weather station**. They work well during a brief time period. Yet they only help people predict the weather for a few hours.

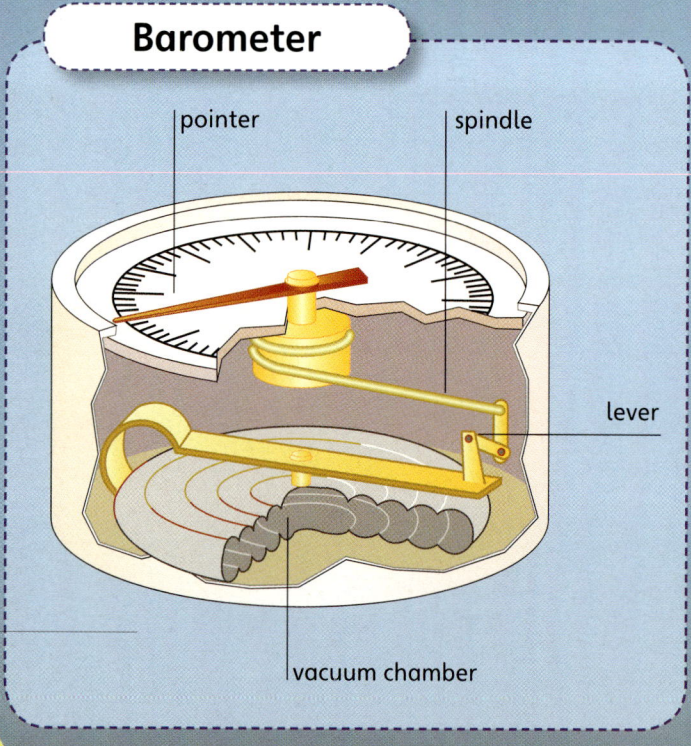

Barometer

pointer
spindle
lever
vacuum chamber

With newer tools, scientists can see weather as it develops hundreds of miles away. They can predict how this distant weather might act when it gets closer. A weather satellite measures temperatures on Earth from space. It can also take photos of clouds. This helps scientists spot and track storms. Doppler radar uses sound waves to detect rain, sleet, hail, and snow. With Doppler radar, a weather forecaster can tell the difference between clouds and rain moving in.

Calculation Station

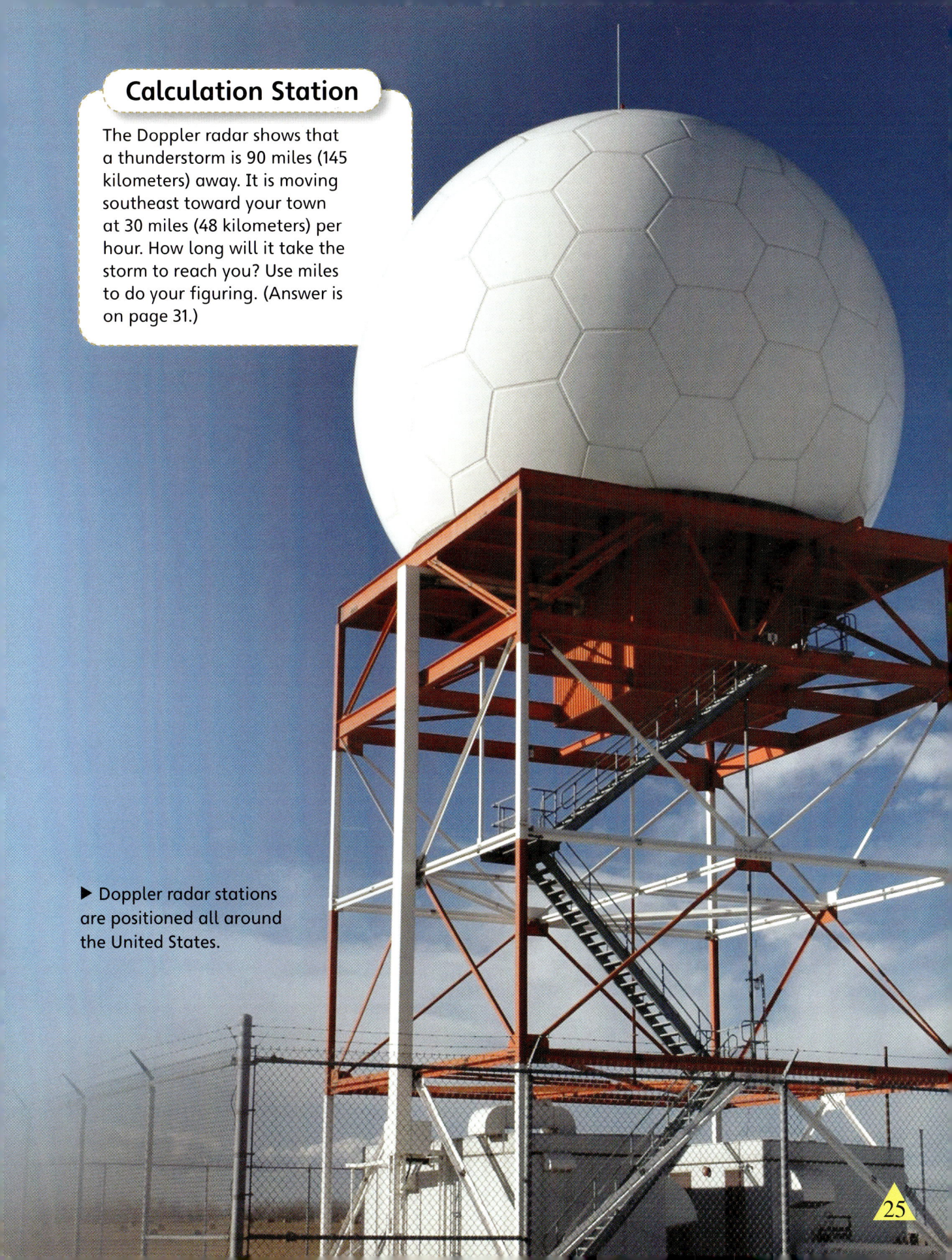

The Doppler radar shows that a thunderstorm is 90 miles (145 kilometers) away. It is moving southeast toward your town at 30 miles (48 kilometers) per hour. How long will it take the storm to reach you? Use miles to do your figuring. (Answer is on page 31.)

▶ Doppler radar stations are positioned all around the United States.

Severe Weather

In severe weather, people take steps to stay safe and protect property. Floods, tornadoes, hurricanes, and winter storms can do damage. So what do people do?

◀ Tornadoes hit the United States about 800 times a year.

Hurricanes, also called typhoons and tropical cyclones, are storms that form over open water and move in a circle. The weakest hurricane has winds of 74 miles (120 kilometers) per hour. These storms can also create storm surges. That is when an ocean creates a wall of water. People protect themselves by building away from areas that can be hit by water. They build strong structures.

Tornadoes are spinning columns of air. They can happen when a warm, moist thunderstorm meets cooler air. Tornadoes can bring winds of up to 250 miles (400 kilometers) an hour. People protect themselves by listening for weather alerts and seeking shelter.

Floods are fast-rising water in low areas. A foot of rainfall in a single area can create floods many feet deep. The high water can last for days and even weeks. People are warned not to drive on flooded streets. When floods threaten, people leave their homes and go to higher ground.

Ice storms can knock down trees as well as phone and electrical lines. Heavy snow can make traveling dangerous. Melting snow can cause flooding. Weather forecasters warn people about dangerous winter weather so they can take precautions to stay safe.

Hands-On Math: Weather Trackers

Research one of the most destructive U.S. storms, the Galveston Hurricane of 1900.

What You Will Need:
- Encyclopedias
- Online reference tools such as http://reference.aol.com, www.encyclopedia.com, education.yahoo.com, encarta.msn.com
- Online search engines such as www.kidsclick.org, www.kids.yahoo.com, and www.askforkids.com

What to Do:

1. Look up the Galveston Hurricane of 1900.

2. Look up Hurricane Alicia, which hit Galveston in 1983.

3. Compare the amount of damage caused by the storms.

Explain Away
Why was the 1900 hurricane so much more destructive than modern-day storms? (Answer is on page 31.)

Weather Myths

People have passed along myths about weather for many years. Have you ever counted seconds after a lightning strike to tell how far away it is? Some people try to tell the temperature by the number of times a cricket chirps. These are common weather myths.

Some of the myths are harmless. Others can cause harm. For example, it is a myth that lightning strikes the tallest object in an area. Lightning instead will strike whatever will help direct electricity to the ground. So someone might stand next to a tall building, thinking he or she is safe. Yet that is not true. People should go inside when there is lightning.

Calculation Station

"Lightning never strikes the same place twice" is a myth. The Empire State Building in New York City is struck about 100 times each year. There are 12 months in a year. Divide 12 into 100 to find the average number of strikes per month. (Answer is on page 31.)

Many people believe the southwest corner of a building is the safest place during a tornado. In 1966, however, a scientist studied tornado damage, and 75 percent of buildings had damage in the southwest corners. Instead of going there, go to the lowest level of the building, away from windows, and get under a bench or mattress if possible.

Nature and nature math have a lot to teach us!

▲ Some people say the number of cricket chirps will tell the weather.

▲ Have you heard the poem, "Red sky in the morning/sailors take warning. Red sky at night/sailors delight"?

Glossary

anemometer Tool that measures wind speed.

barometer Tool that measures air pressure.

crystal Solid form of a substance that makes the same shape for the same substance.

Doppler radar Tool that looks at space to measure precipitation.

Fibonacci Mathematician who lived from the late twelfth to early thirteenth century.

Fibonacci sequence Special pattern of numbers Fibonacci saw in nature, in which each number is the sum of the two numbers before it: 1, 1, 2, 3, 5, 8, 13, . . .

hygrometer Tool that measures humidity in the air.

molecule Smallest unit of a compound that still has the properties of that compound when on its own.

pattern Something that is repeated in a similar way.

probability The chance of an event happening.

rain gauge Tool that measures the amount of rainfall.

reflectional symmetry When an object or an animal has two sides that are mirror images of each other, if its whole image were divided in two.

regular hexagon A shape with six sides that are the same length and six angles of the same measure.

regular polygon Polygon, or flat shape, with sides all the same length and angles all the same measure.

rotational symmetry When an object or an animal looks the same after some amount of rotation.

satellite Tool in space that measures light and temperature.

spiral Shape circling around a central point.

symmetry When size, shape, and arrangement of different sides of something look the same.

tessellation Design created by repeating the same shape, without gaps or overlaps.

weather station Collection of tools (anemometer, air gauge, hygrometer, barometer, and thermometer) used to measure weather.

Answer Key
Calculation Station

p. 4: To find the pattern, add the previous two numbers in the sequence; 13, 21, 34, 55.

p. 9: The fourth, fifth, and sixth turns are 13, 21, 34.

p. 13: There are 8 clockwise spirals and 13 counterclockwise spirals.

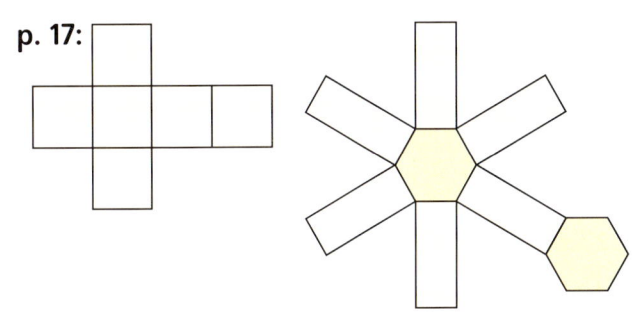

p. 17:

p. 19: Snowflakes will vary. The filter must be folded in thirds in order to get six sections. Folding the filter in half again would result in a four-section snowflake.

p. 21: Examples of reflectional symmetry might include a blade of grass, a seed, and leaves from trees and shrubs. Examples of rotational symmetry might include a flower head, a pine cone, and a fruit.

p. 25: 90 divided by 30 is 3 hours.

p. 28: 100 divided by 12 is 8.3.

Hands-On Math

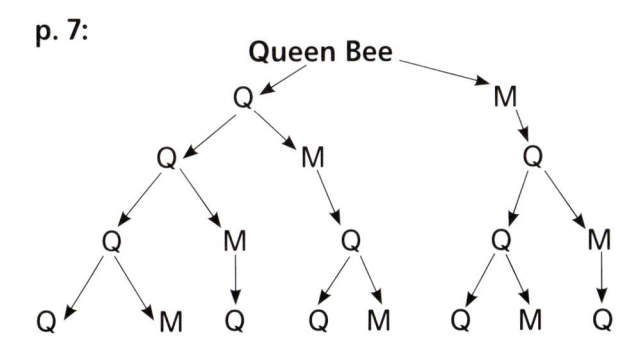

p. 7:

Queen Bee

The numbers are also part of the Fibonacci sequence.

p. 11: All plants listed have sections inside that are Fibonacci numbers. Examples of other plants that use Fibonacci numbers are clovers that have three leaves and maple leaves that have five lobes.

p. 15: Tessellations vary depending on the cuts made. Pieces fit together only by sliding the piece up, down, left, or right. Flipping or turning will not create a "fit."

p. 19: The filter must be folded in thirds in order to get six sections. Folding the filter in half again would result in a four-section snowflake.

p. 23: Temperatures will vary depending on the season and climate. Predictions should follow the trend of the temperatures recorded on Days 1 through 7.

p. 27: Even though there were probably more homes in 1983, there were fewer homes destroyed because builders now know better how to make buildings to handle the wind and water damage.

Index

anemometer, 24
banana, 10
butterfly, 20
claw, 20
compound, 16
crystal, 16, 17, 18
cube, 17
Doppler radar, 24, 25
emerald, 16, 17, 18
Fibonacci, 4
Fibonacci sequence, 5, 6, 7, 8, 9, 10, 11, 12
fiddler crab, 20
flood, 26
forecast, 22, 23, 24, 26
gold, 16, 17
hexagon, 14, 17, 18
hive, 6
honeybee, 6, 14
honeycomb, 14
human, 20
hurricane, 26, 27
hygrometer, 24
ice crystal, 18
ice storm, 26
mathematician, 4, 9, 10

molecule, 16
myth, 28
pattern, 4, 6, 8, 9, 11, 12, 14, 20, 22
pineapple, 12
plate, 18
polygon, 14
probability, 22
queen, 6, 7
rabbit, 4, 5
rain gauge, 24
reflectional symmetry, 20, 21
rings, 14
rotational symmetry, 20, 21
royal jelly, 6
satellite, 24
sneezewort, 8, 9
snowflake, 18, 19
spiral, 12, 13
square, 15, 17
starfish, 20
sunflower, 8, 12, 13
tessellation, 14, 15, 16
thermometer, 23, 24
three-dimensional, 16, 17, 19
tornado, 26, 29
weather station, 24

dabble lab

Manga Drawing with
DC

HOW TO DRAW BATMAN MANGA!

by Christopher Harbo

illustrated by Haining

Batman created by Bob Kane with Bill Finger

raintree
a Capstone company — publishers for children

Raintree is an imprint of Capstone Global Library Limited, a company incorporated in England and Wales having its registered office at 264 Banbury Road, Oxford, OX2 7DY – Registered company number: 6695582

www.raintree.co.uk
myorders@raintree.co.uk

Copyright © 2024 DC.
BATMAN and all related characters and elements © & ™ DC. (s24)

All rights reserved. No part of this publication may be reproduced in any form or by any means (including photocopying or storing it in any medium by electronic means and whether or not transiently or incidentally to some other use of this publication) without the written permission of the copyright owner, except in accordance with the provisions of the Copyright, Designs and Patents Act 1988 or under the terms of a licence issued by the Copyright Licensing Agency, 5th Floor, Shackleton House, 4 Battle Bridge Lane, London SE1 2HX (www.cla.co.uk). Applications for the copyright owner's written permission should be addressed to the publisher.

Edited by Abby Huff
Designed by Hilary Wacholz
Picture research by Jo Miller
Production by Tori Abraham
Originated by Capstone Global Library Ltd

978 1 3982 5370 4 (hardback)
978 1 3982 5374 2 (paperback)

British Library Cataloguing in Publication Data
A full catalogue record for this book is available from the British Library.

Acknowledgements
Photos: Capstone Studio: Karon Dubke 5 (all), Backgrounds and design elements: Capstone

The publisher and the author shall not be liable for any damages allegedly arising from the information in this book, and they specifically disclaim any liability from the use or application of any of the contents of this book.

Printed and bound in India

CONTENTS

LEAP INTO MANGA! 4

THE MANGAKA'S TOOLKIT 5

BATMAN 6

ROBIN 8

BATGIRL 10

BATWING 12

BATWOMAN 14

CATWOMAN 16

THE JOKER 18

HARLEY QUINN 20

THE RIDDLER 22

POISON IVY 24

THE PENGUIN 26

BATMAN VS CLAYFACE 28

LEAP INTO MANGA!

Batman has battled to keep the mean streets of Gotham City clean of crime for more than 80 years. In that time, his daring feats have come to life in comic books, TV shows and mega-hit films. But did you know the Dark Knight once made a giant leap across the Pacific Ocean? It's true! In 1966, *Batman* by Jiro Kuwata featured the Caped Crusader as he'd never been seen before — in Japanese manga!

What is manga? Simply put, it's comics and graphic novels from Japan. While the manga art style dates back more than 800 years, its popularity in books and magazines really exploded in the late 1940s. Since then, manga has become famous for its awesome art. Manga characters have large eyes, small noses and mouths, and pointed chins. And when it comes to heart-pounding action and dynamic scenes, few comics match manga's electric look. It's no wonder manga mania has spread all over the world!

SO DON'T WAIT ANOTHER SECOND! TAKE YOUR OWN GIANT LEAP BY REUNITING BATMAN WITH THE MANGA WORLD. DRAW YOUR FAVOURITE GOTHAM CITY HEROES AND VILLAINS IN MANGA STYLE!

THE MANGAKA'S TOOLKIT

All manga artists — or mangaka — need the right tools to make amazing art. Gather the following supplies before you begin drawing:

PAPER
Art supply and hobby shops have many types of special drawing paper. But any blank, unlined paper will work well too.

PENCILS
Sketch in pencil first. That way, if you make a mistake or need to change a detail, it's easy to rub out and redraw.

PENCIL SHARPENER
Keep a good pencil sharpener within reach. Sharp pencils will help you draw clean lines.

ERASERS
Making mistakes is a normal part of drawing. Ordinary pencil erasers work in a pinch. But high-quality rubber or kneaded erasers last longer and won't damage your paper.

BLACK MARKER PENS
When your sketch is finished, trace over the final lines with a black marker pen. By "inking" the lines, your characters will practically leap off the page!

COLOURED PENCILS AND MARKERS
While manga stories are usually created in black and white, they often have full-colour covers. Feel free to complete your manga masterpiece with coloured pencils and markers. There's nothing like a pop of colour to bring characters to life!

BATMAN

When the Bat-Signal blazes over Gotham City, the Dark Knight always answers the call. Leaping into action, he follows the clues to track down the world's worst Super-Villains. And when he finds his foes, the Caped Crusader grabs a Batarang from his Utility Belt, then lets it fly with a flick of the wrist!

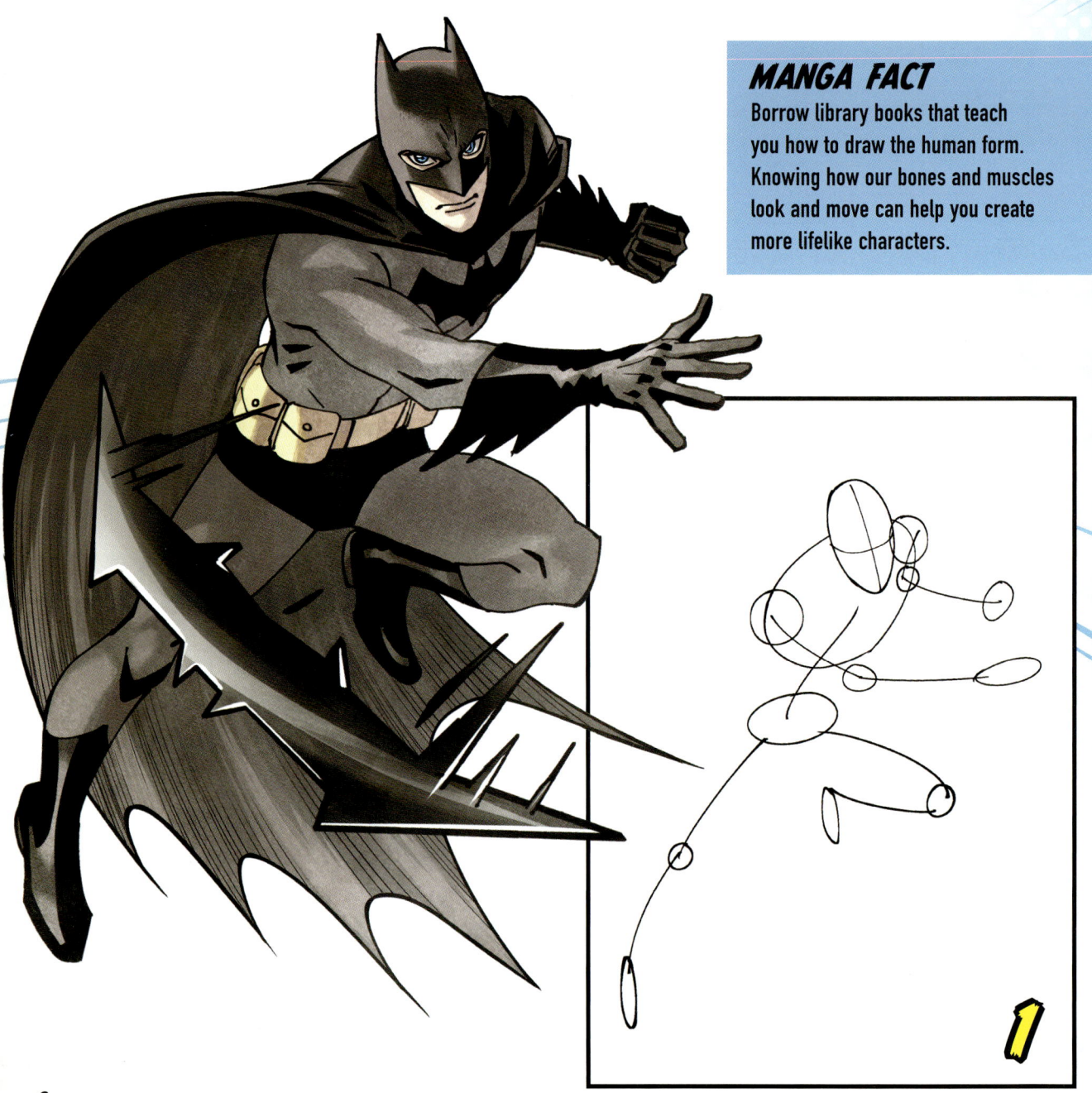

MANGA FACT
Borrow library books that teach you how to draw the human form. Knowing how our bones and muscles look and move can help you create more lifelike characters.

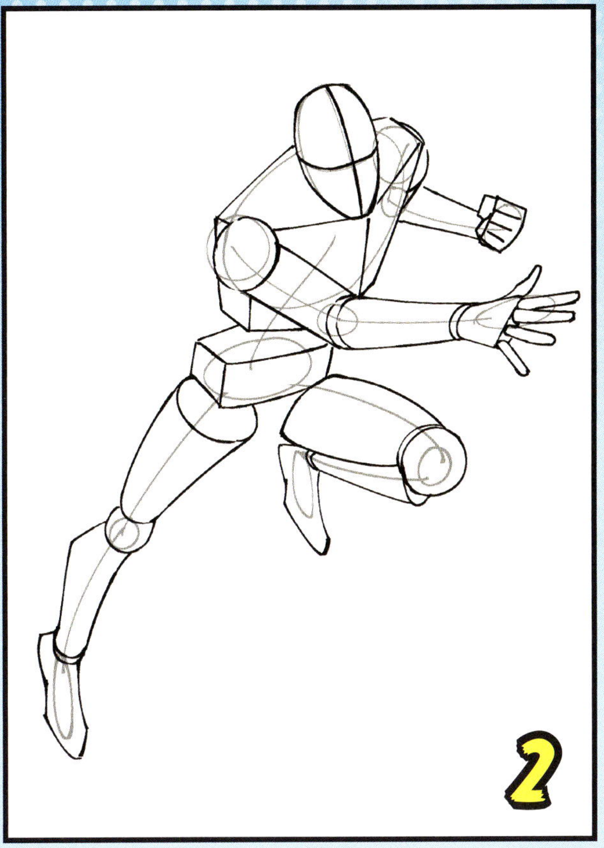
2

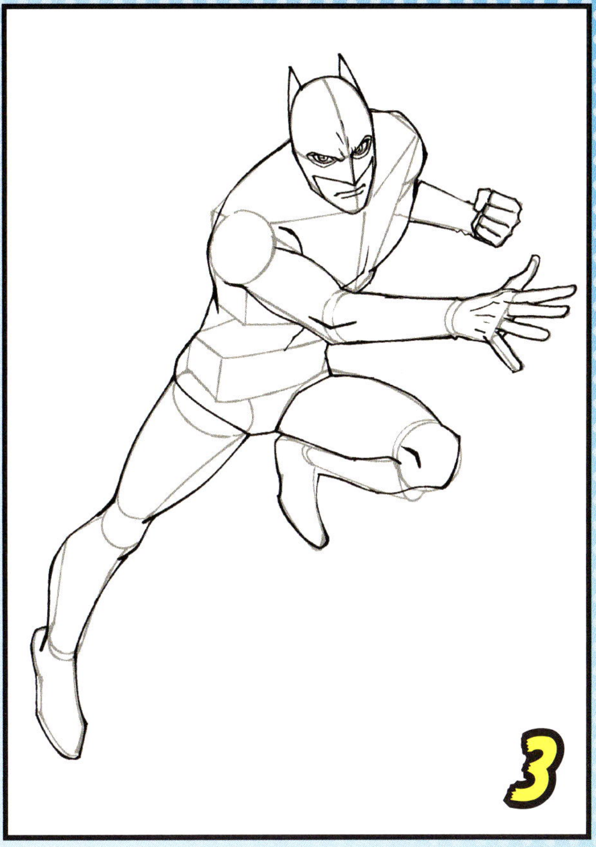
3

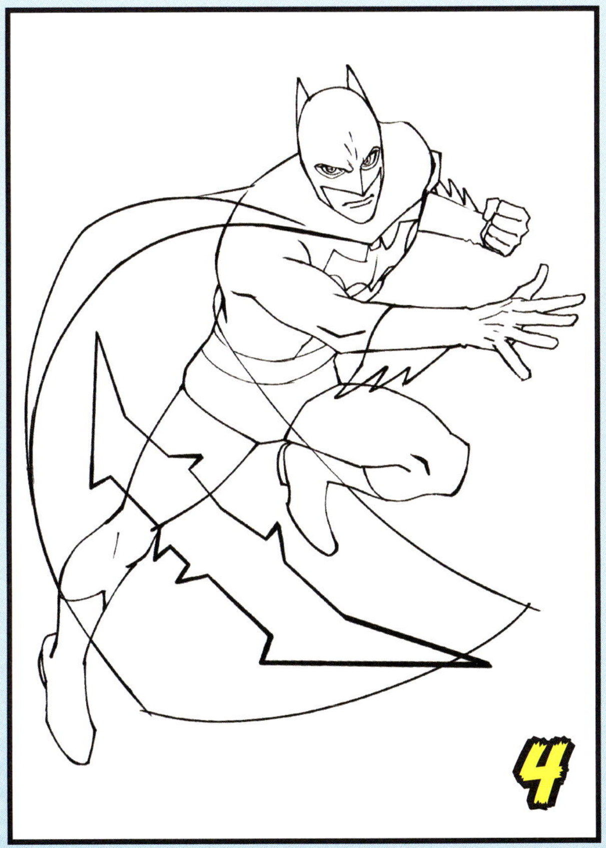
4

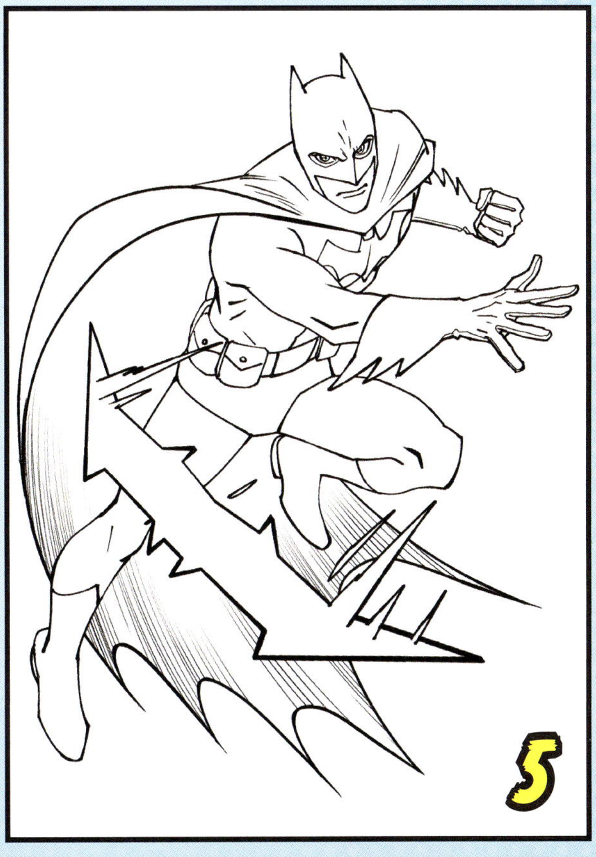
5

ROBIN

Few Super Hero sidekicks compare to Robin. His lightning-fast reflexes and quick wit are more than a match for any of Batman's baddies. Best of all, Robin is loyal and true. Whenever the Caped Crusader gets in a bind, he can count on the Boy Wonder to swoop down on a Batrope in the nick of time!

1

MANGA FACT
Manga is read right to left. That's because Japanese is read that way too. Instead of flipping the pages of original manga, English-language versions often keep them as is, to avoid affecting the art.

2

3

4

5

BATGIRL

Batgirl isn't about to let the Dynamic Duo have all the fun. Each night, this tech-savvy teen patrols Gotham City for cold-hearted criminals. Will tonight be the night she hunts down Harley Quinn or rounds up the Riddler? Either way, this martial arts master is bound to have a blast kicking crime to the kerb!

1

MANGA FACT
Speed lines often surround manga characters during action scenes to add excitement. Draw speed lines behind Batgirl to give her kick extra oomph!

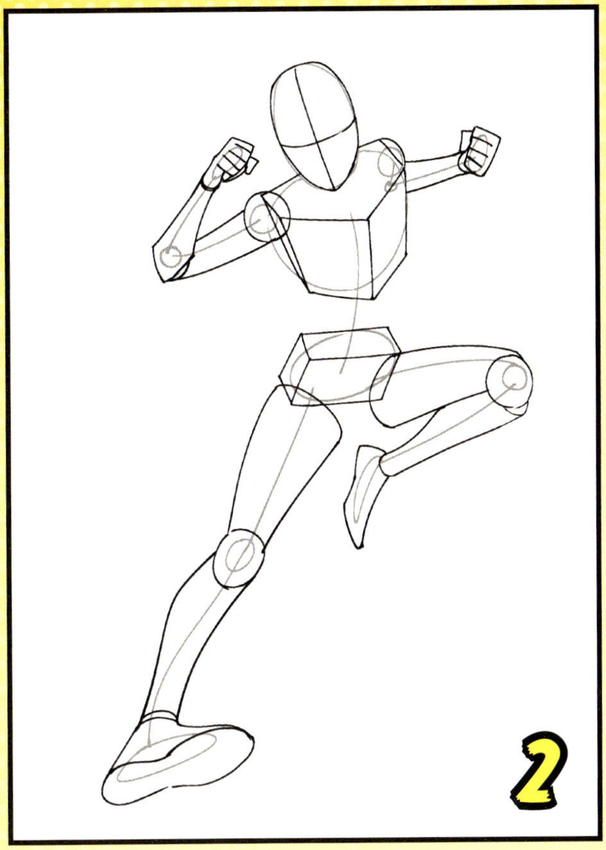
2

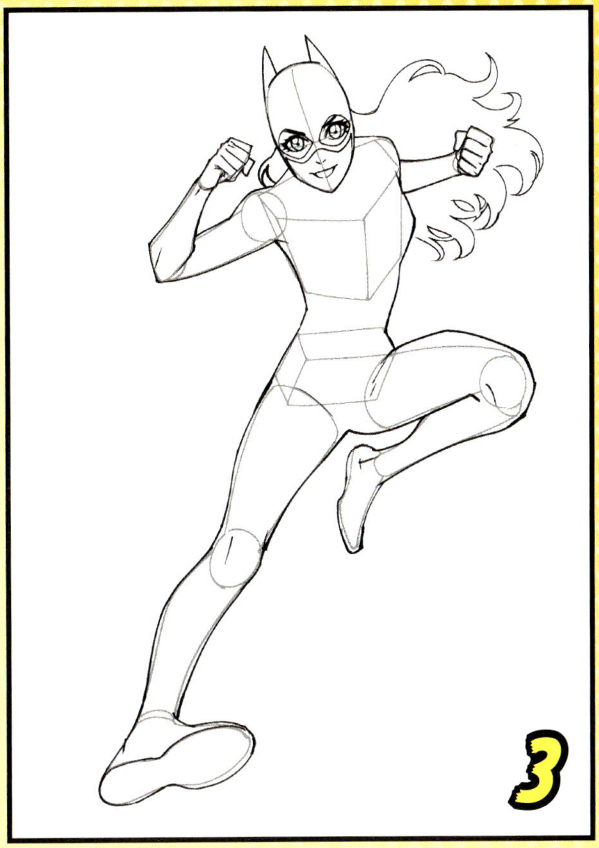
3

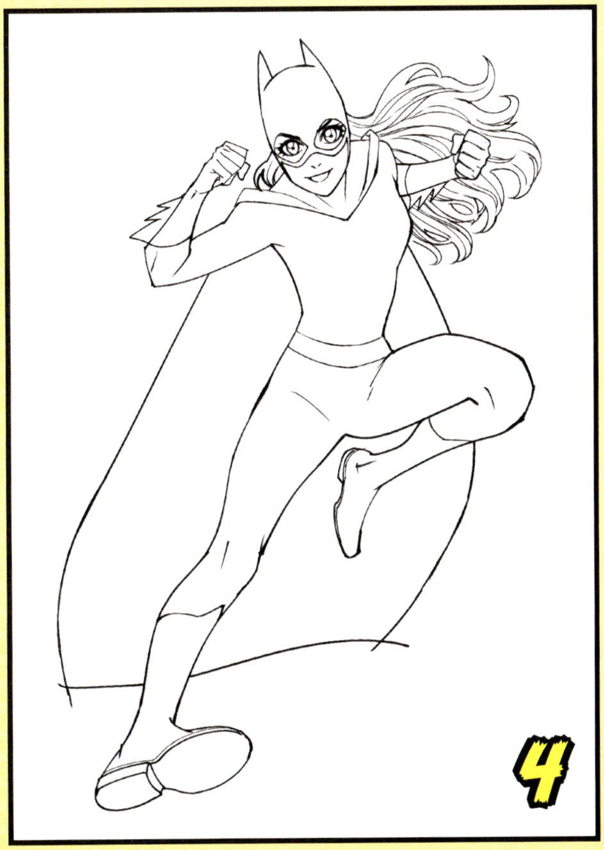
4

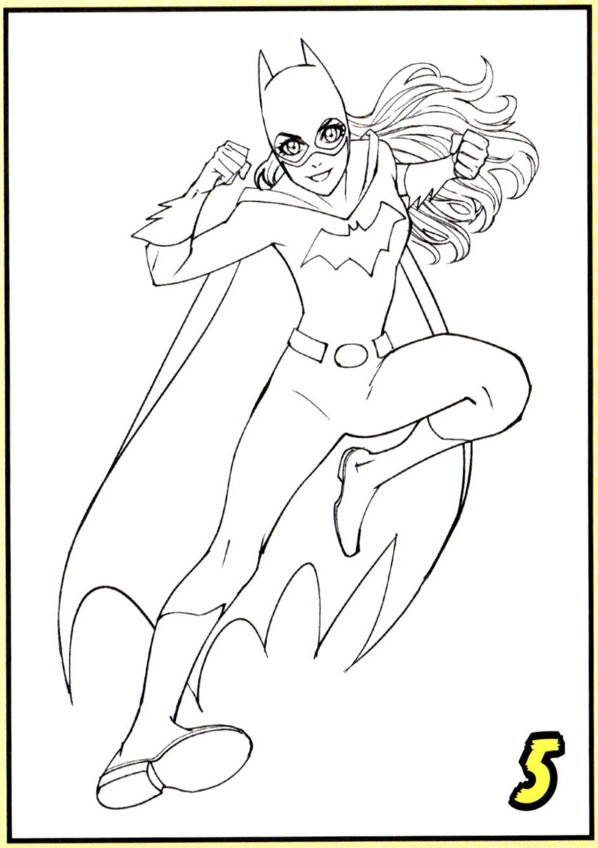
5

BATWING

Luke Fox is an expert boxer and mixed martial artist. But he knows it takes more than muscle to fight crime. So the son of Wayne Enterprises CEO Lucius Fox also harnesses the power of technology. Donning an advanced Batsuit of his father's design, Luke glides into action as Batwing!

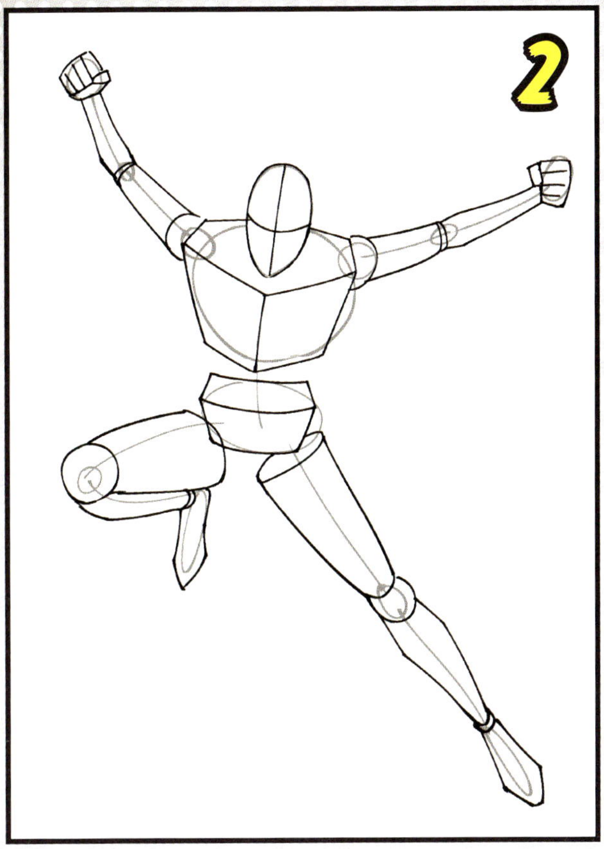
2

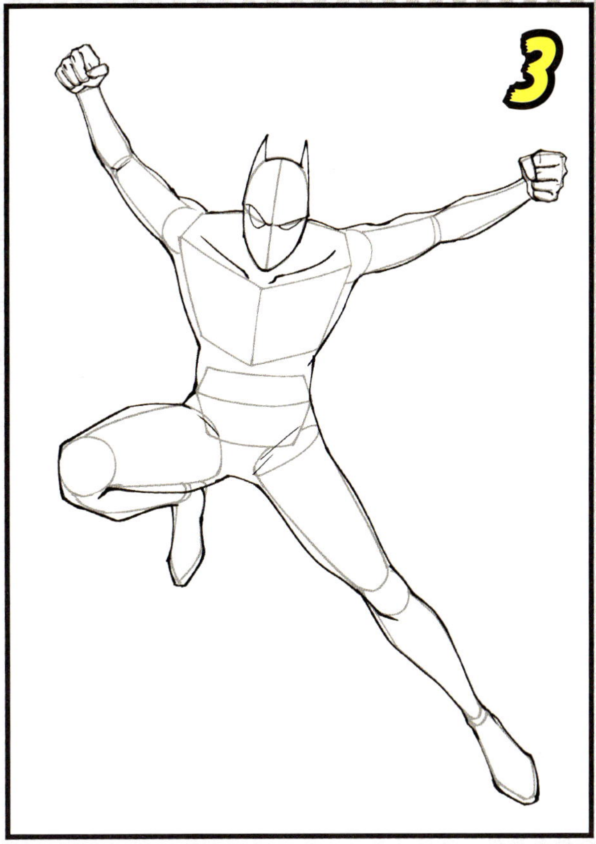
3

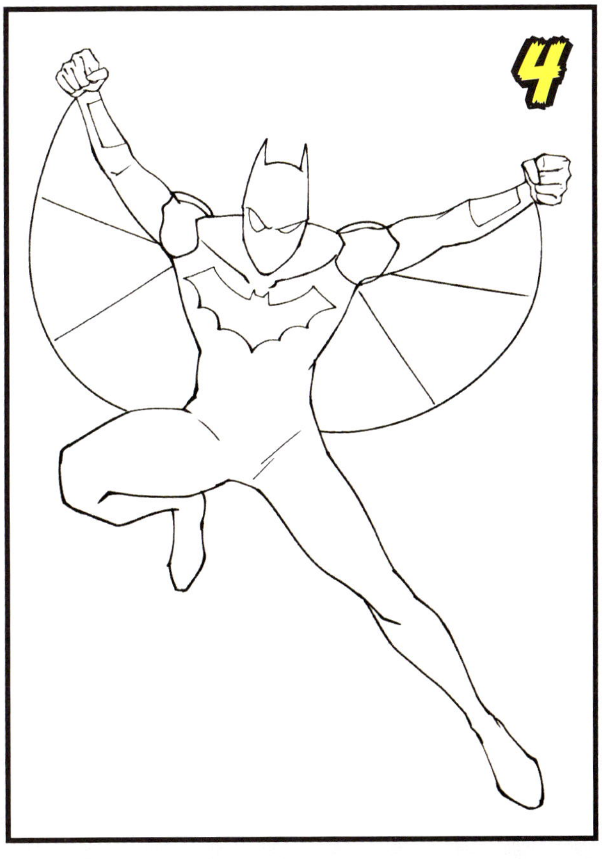
4

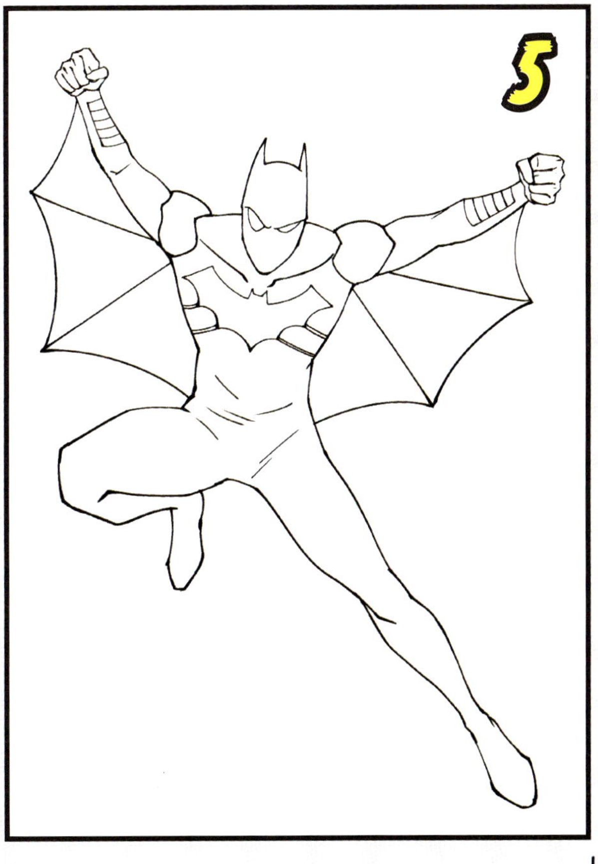
5

BATWOMAN

Kate Kane proves crime fighting runs in the family — the Bat Family. She's a cousin of Bruce Wayne, aka Batman. She's also a dedicated defender of Gotham City. Disguised as Batwoman, she relies on her keen mind and superior combat skills every time she charges fearlessly into a fight!

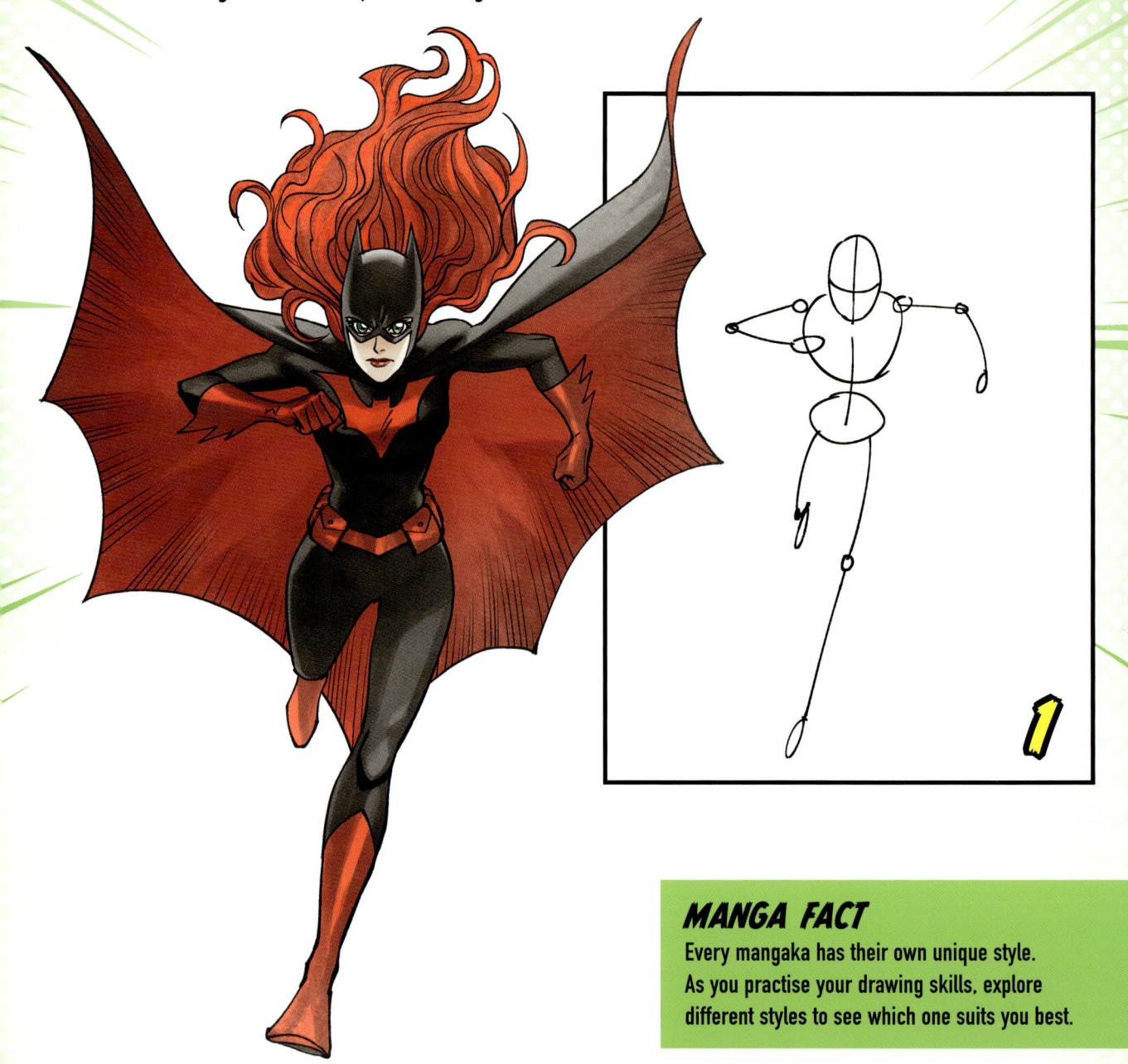

1

MANGA FACT
Every mangaka has their own unique style. As you practise your drawing skills, explore different styles to see which one suits you best.

15

CATWOMAN

This professional thief is a bit of a *purr*-fectionist. With feline grace and agility, Catwoman can slink her way into just about any museum gallery or bank vault. But don't think that cracking safes is her only skill. She's also a cunning fighter who isn't afraid to crack her whip!

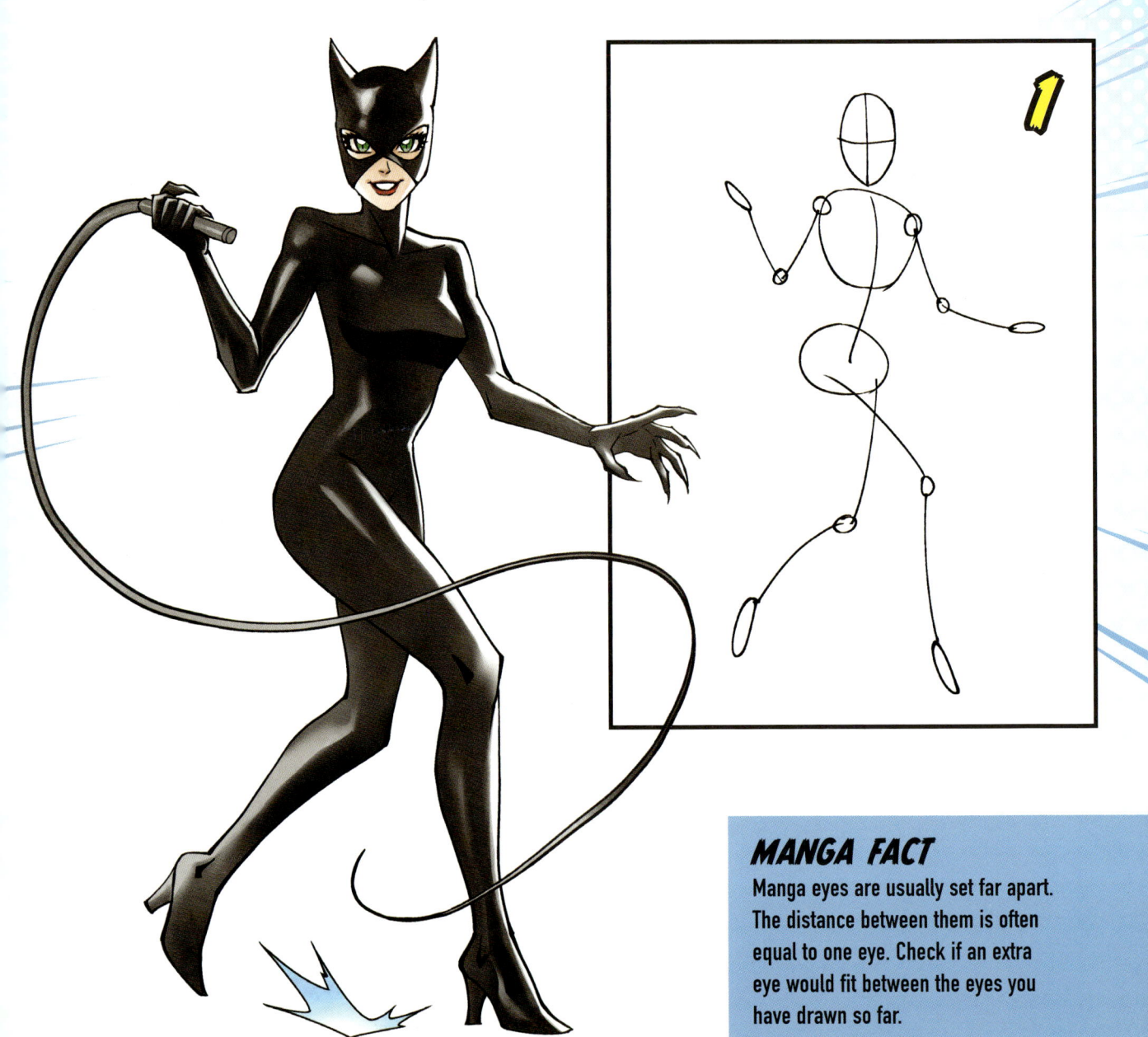

1

MANGA FACT
Manga eyes are usually set far apart. The distance between them is often equal to one eye. Check if an extra eye would fit between the eyes you have drawn so far.

2

3

4

5

THE JOKER

The Joker is Batman's greatest enemy — and a treacherous trickster. From Joker Toxin in his lapel flower to a shocking hand buzzer, the Clown Prince of Crime always has a trick up his sleeve. So look out! Those playing cards are as razor-sharp as his criminal mind!

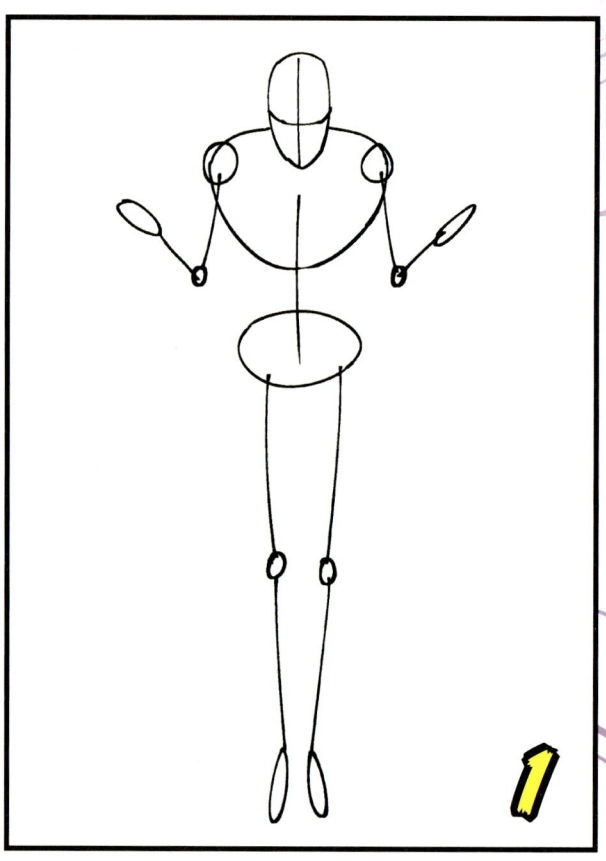

MANGA FACT
In Japan, shōnen manga is geared towards boys. Shōjo manga is aimed at girls. But boys and girls often read both.

19

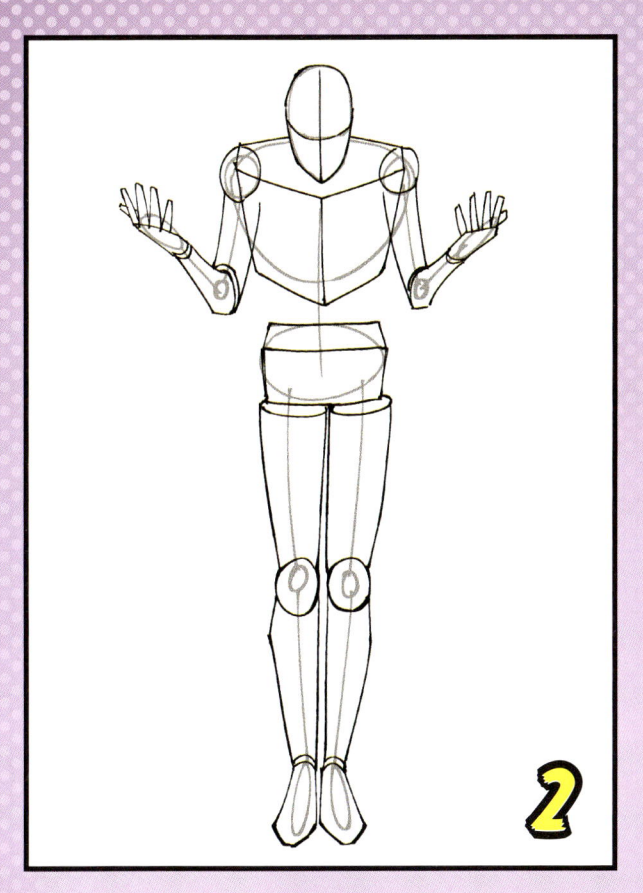

HARLEY QUINN

Harley Quinn may be a jester, but she's nobody's fool. The Clown Princess of Crime knows what she wants — lots and lots of money! And you can bet she's going to have a hoot while grabbing the loot. With her huge mallet in hand, Harley has a smashing good time!

1

MANGA FACT
Chibis are short, cute characters with large heads and tiny bodies. Imagine Harley as a chibi and try drawing her in that style!

21

THE RIDDLER

Why would a cunning criminal leave clever clues for a caped crime fighter to crack? For this rascal of riddles, the answer is elementary: Why not? Armed with his question mark cane and a wily wit, the Riddler loves nothing more than to baffle Batman!

1

2

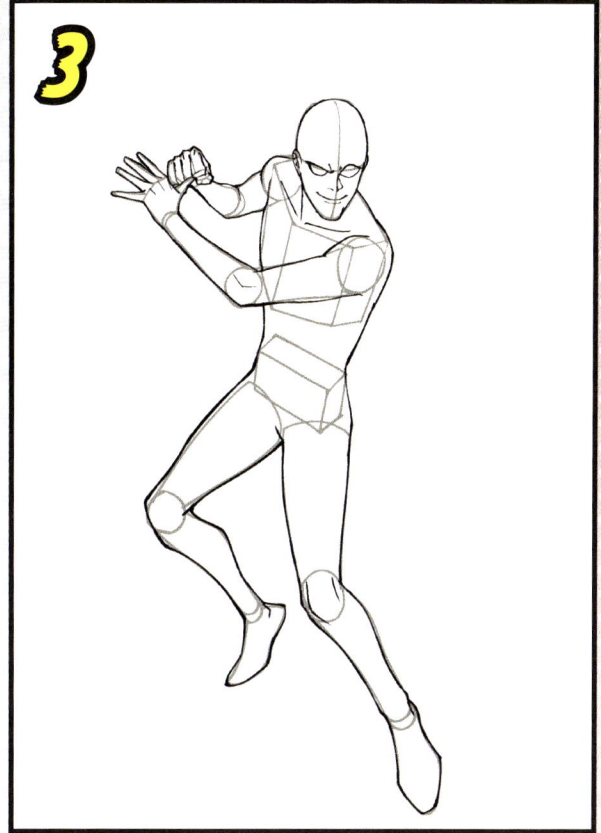

3

4

5

23

POISON IVY

1

Make way for the Queen of Green! Using just her mind, Poison Ivy commands plants to carry out her wicked whims. From venomous Venus flytraps to vicious vines, this villain's fearsome flora can ensnare even the most daring do-gooders!

25

THE PENGUIN

The Penguin is a criminal kingpin who's as proud as a peacock. He's always dressed for success when pulling off his plots. With his trademark top hat, monocle and tuxedo, the self-proclaimed "Gentleman of Crime" certainly looks the part. But beware this bad bird's tricky umbrella — or your goose is cooked!

1

MANGA FACT
Manga series feature more than just super heroes and action adventures. From history and sport to fantasy and comedy, manga has many types of stories for everyone to enjoy.

27

BATMAN VS CLAYFACE

As Clayface rampages through the streets, Batman springs into action. Will the shape-shifting villain's twisted tentacle send the Dark Knight flying? Or can the Caped Crusader bring this muddy menace to justice? AS THE MANGAKA, THE FATE OF GOTHAM CITY IS IN YOUR HANDS!

1

MANGA FACT
Osamu Tezuka is often called the "Godfather of Manga". During his career, he created more than 170,000 pages of manga! *Astro Boy* and *Princess Knight* were among his most popular.

29

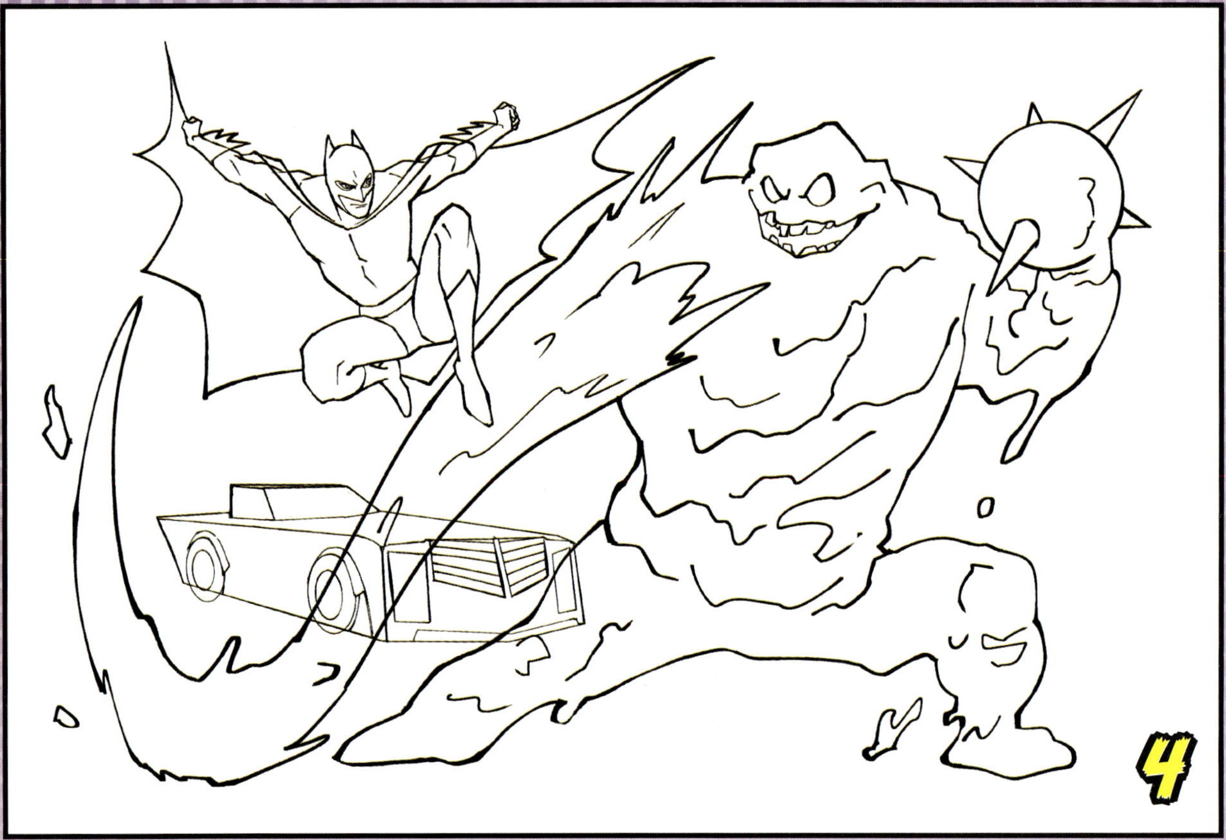
4

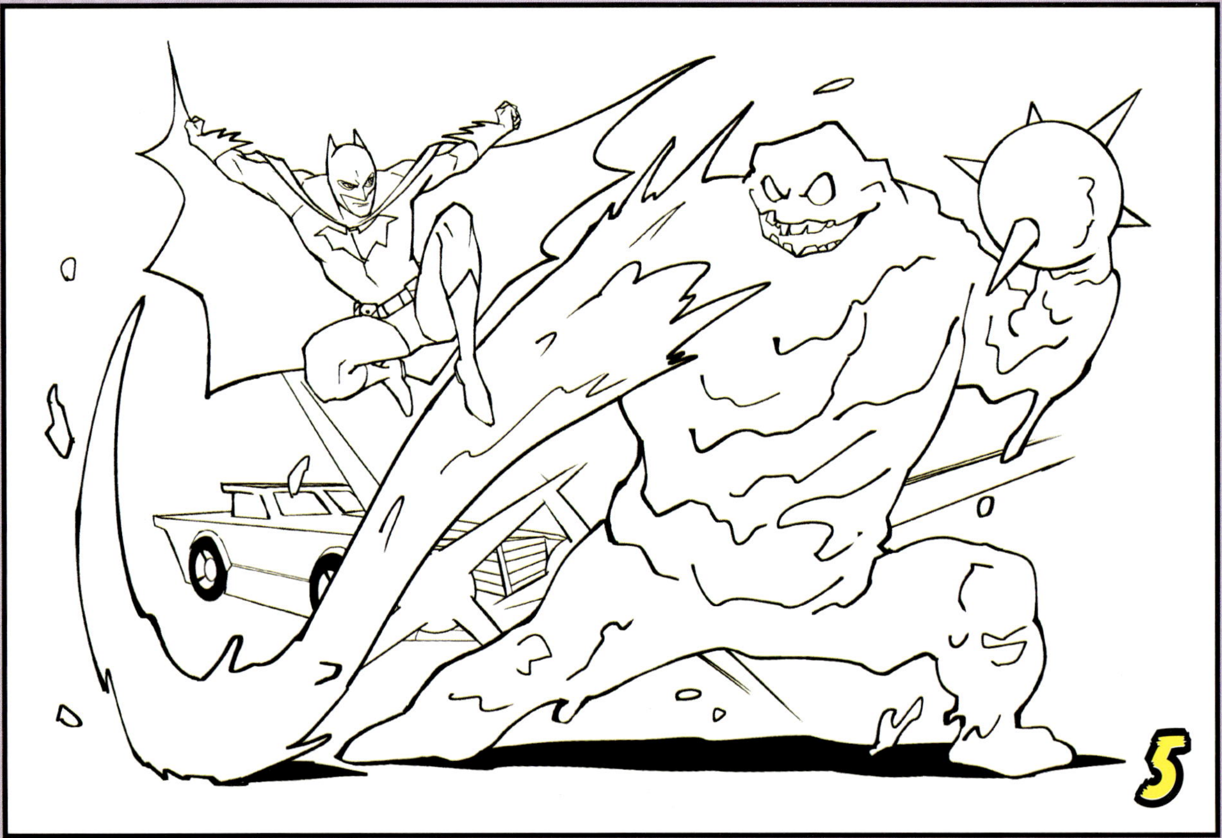
5

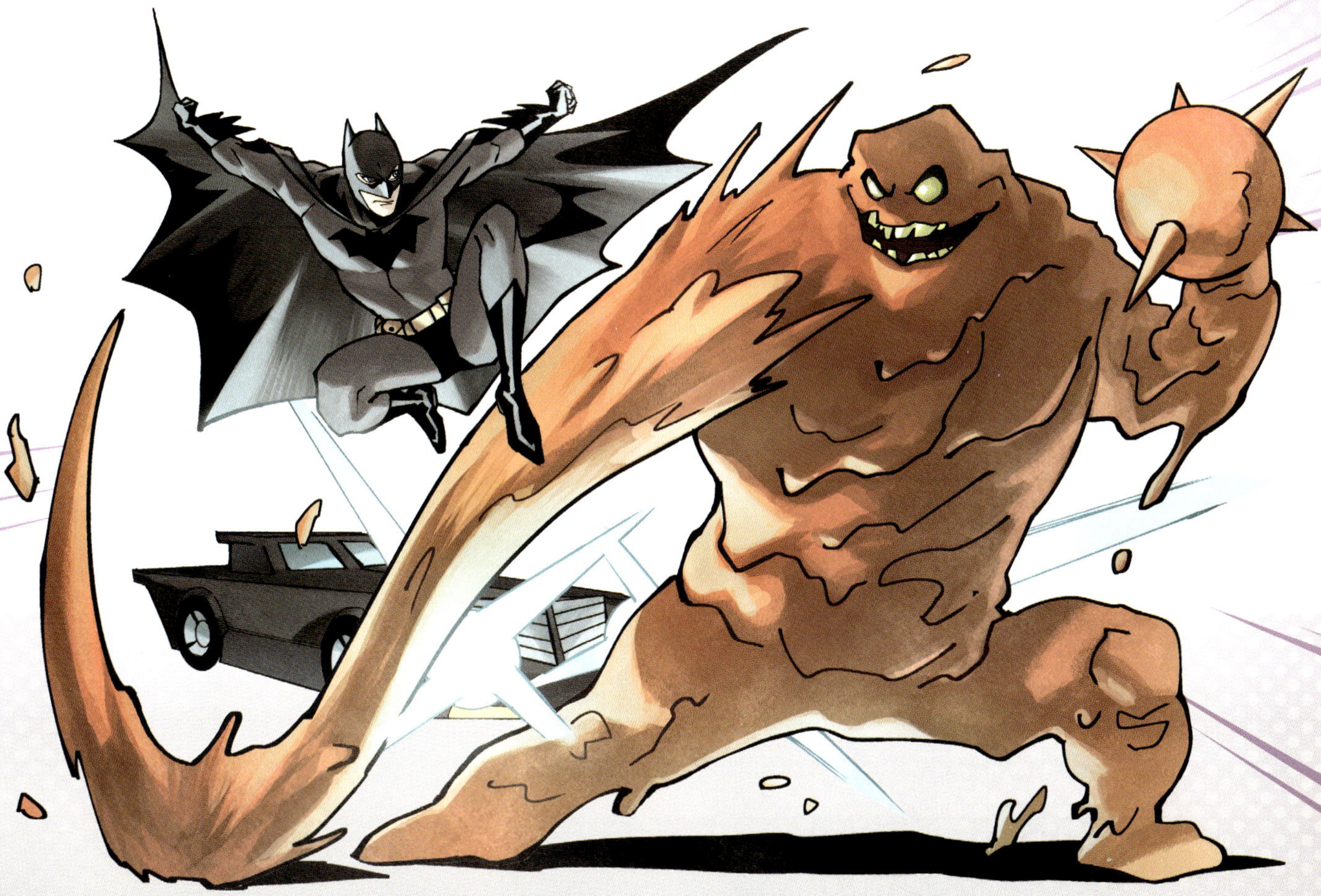

MORE DC SUPER HERO FUN!

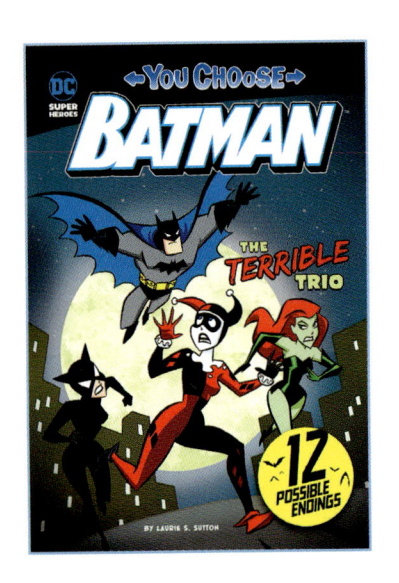

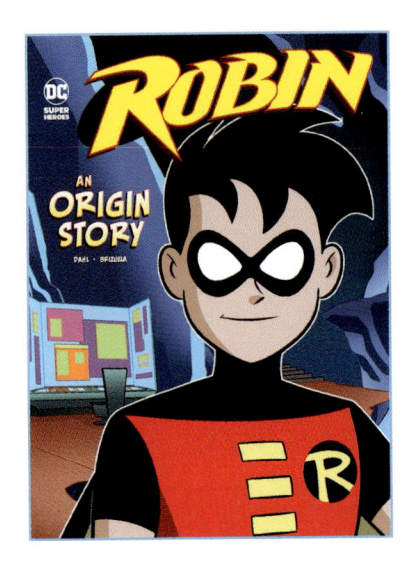

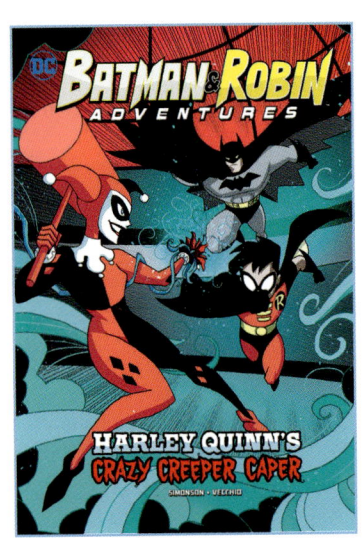

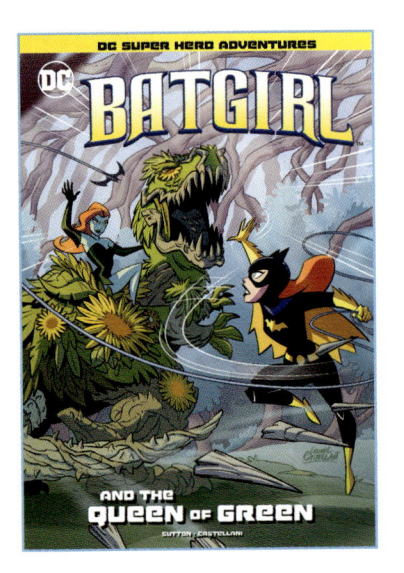